Empire of Mystery

PRICE STERN SLOAN
Los Angeles

Trade Routes

When Marco Polo was born in 1254, Venice, his home city, was becoming the wealthiest city in Europe. This came from Venice's control of the European end of the valuable spice and silk trade that came across Asia from China and the Far East. When these goods arrived at the eastern Mediterranean, they were brought to Venice in Venetian ships. From Venice, they were exported to other parts of Europe.

The Venetians, and the rest of Europe, knew little about the mysterious lands where these goods originated. The cargoes changed hands often as they crossed Asia. The Venetians only handled the last lap of the trade.

When Marco Polo was a boy, his father, Nicolo, used to go to Sudak, on the Black Sea in Russia, to trade in goods that had come across Asia along the route known as the Silk Road.

Nicolo's trips to Sudak usually took two or three months. But in 1260, when Marco was six, Nicolo Polo and his brother Maffeo left Venice for Sudak and did not return for nine years.

At Sudak, some Russian merchants tell of good trading to be had elsewhere. They will share their secret if Nicolo and Maffeo can say where these cargoes come from. Set **Super Q** *to Mode* **4B** *and see if you can guess their origins. You may make only two mistakes.*

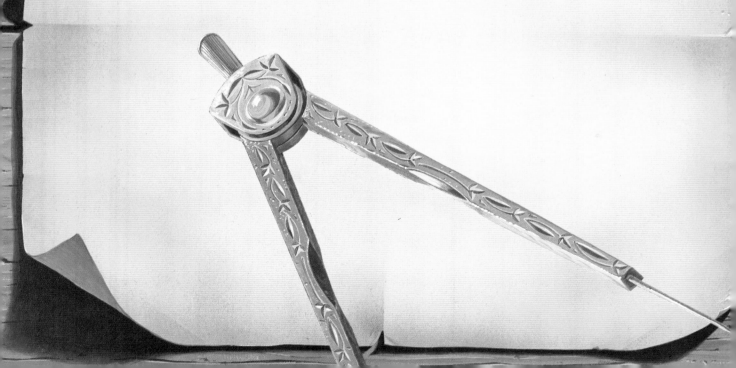

SAUDI ARABIA

THAILAND

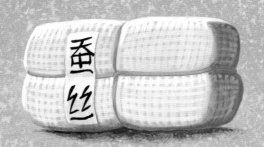

CHINA

VIETNAM

TURKEY

GREECE

ALASKA

IRELAND

FRANCE

GERMANY

SCANDINAVIA

HOLLAND

INDIA

PERU

BOLIVIA

SPAIN

PERSIA

ISRAEL

RUSSIA

YUGOSLAVIA

START

To China and Back

The Russians told the brothers to travel further east to Bokhara, beyond the Caspian Sea. Once they had traded there, Nicolo and Maffeo had originally intended to return home, but instead continued eastwards.

After meeting some Chinese merchants, Nicolo and Maffeo eventually reached Peking, capital of China. The Mongol emperor of China, Kublai Khan, welcomed the brothers. They were the first Europeans he had seen, and he was curious to know about their homeland and its customs.

Kublai asked the Polos to return home with a letter for the pope. The letter requested the pope to send some learned monks to explain Christianity, and also some holy oil from the Church of the Holy Sepulchre in Jerusalem.

After a three-year journey, Nicolo and Maffeo arrived at the Mediterranean, only to hear that the pope had died and that the next pope had not yet been chosen. How could they deliver Kublai Khan's letter? They asked the papal legate in Acre, Priest Theobald, who said there was nothing but to wait for a new pope.

The Polos went back to Venice to see their families. Nicolo's wife had died, and his son Marco, now 15, was living with relatives.

After two years, there was still no pope. Nicolo and Maffeo decided to return to China anyway, taking Marco with them. They set off together in 1271.

Nicolo and Maffeo's first journey to Peking was long and hard. On their return with Marco, they will be better prepared for some of the dangers.

*Set **Super Q** to Mode **4H** and spot along the safe route avoiding any of the hazards. Be careful: you have only five lives.*

FINISH

The Mission

The Polos stopped at Acre, where the papal legate gave them permission to collect the holy oil from Jerusalem. There, they heard that the legate had been chosen as the new pope, Gregory X. They returned to Acre and Gregory (who had not yet left for Rome) gave them two very learned monks, Brother Nicholas and Brother William, to accompany them to China.

The party then sailed to Ayas, the start of the overland route to Persia. News came of fighting on the route. The monks were too frightened to go on, so the Polos had to continue alone.

Their route took them northeast through Armenia and Turkey to Georgia, and then looped southwest to Baghdad. From there, the Polos travelled east into Persia as far as Kerman, where they turned south to reach Hormuz, on the Persian Gulf.

*Set **Super Q** to Mode 6A and follow the correct path in the flagstones to answer the question: What was the name and title of Gregory X before he became pope?*

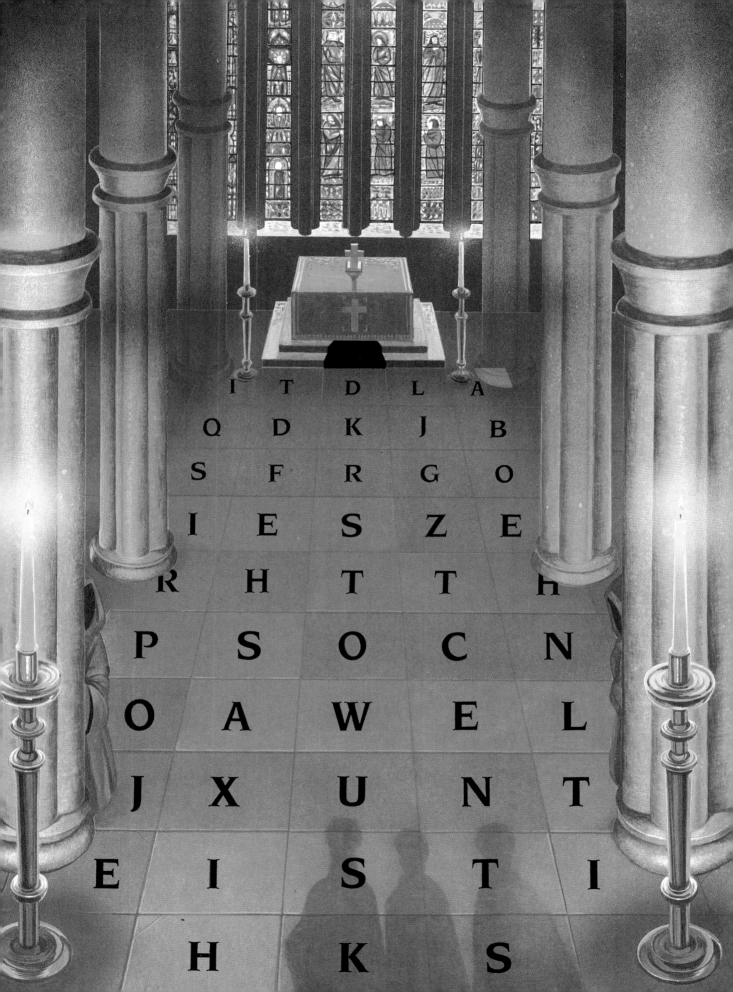

A Jewelled City

For Marco, everything was strange and new. The hardships of the journey did not prevent him from carefully noting all that he saw and learning as much as he could about the peoples they met.

In Armenia, he was told about a square-shaped, snow-capped mountain on which Noah's Ark was said to have come to rest after the Flood. This was Mount Ararat.

Near the Georgian border, Marco saw a spring from which a stream of oil gushed. This oil, he reported, was not good to eat, but was used to burn in lamps and as an ointment for people and camels suffering from itch or scab.

Turning south, the travellers came to the fabled city of Baghdad, which Marco described as "the largest and most splendid city in all these parts". Baghdad was famous for its fabrics woven from gold and silk, richly decorated with birds and animals. To Baghdad came merchants from the Indian Ocean, with pearls. These were pierced in Baghdad for export to Europe.

Journeying east to Persia, the Polos came to Saveh, from where the Three Kings were said to have set off to worship the newborn Christ. Marco wrote that their bodies were still preserved in Saveh, with hair and beads, each in its own sepulchre.

Marco is admiring the sights when he knocks a leather purse from the hands of a burly merchant, spilling pearls all over the floor ... Set **Super Q** to Mode **8C** and, in 45 seconds, find a route across the tiles without stepping on any pearls. Be quick. The merchant is wielding a nasty dagger ...

只

Y

START

FINISH

Attacked!

Next the travellers arrived at Kerman. From here, travellers to China could either take the northern route over India or they could turn south to Hormuz and travel by sea.

The Polos decided to go to Hormuz with a caravan of merchants. As they crossed the Plain of Rudbar, they were attacked by a band of robber people called Karaunas. Marco wrote that these people used magic to turn the day dark, so their victims could not see them coming.

The three Venetians finally arrived at the busy port of Hormuz, where ships arrived from India carrying spices, precious stones, pearls, silk and gold cloth, elephants' tusks and many other goods.

The Polos did not like the look of the ships at Hormuz. Marco wrote "their ships are very bad, and many founder, because they are not fastened with iron nails but stitched together with thread made from coconut husks".

So the travellers decided to return to Kerman and take the overland route to China. From Kerman, they continued northwards through wild, barren country to the borders of Persia.

Set **Super Q** to Mode **8B**. Help the Polos escape the Karauna robbers along the hidden route through the smoke. You have only 30 seconds to reach safety in the nearby city of Kamasal. If you find this too hard, use Modes **8C** or **8D**.

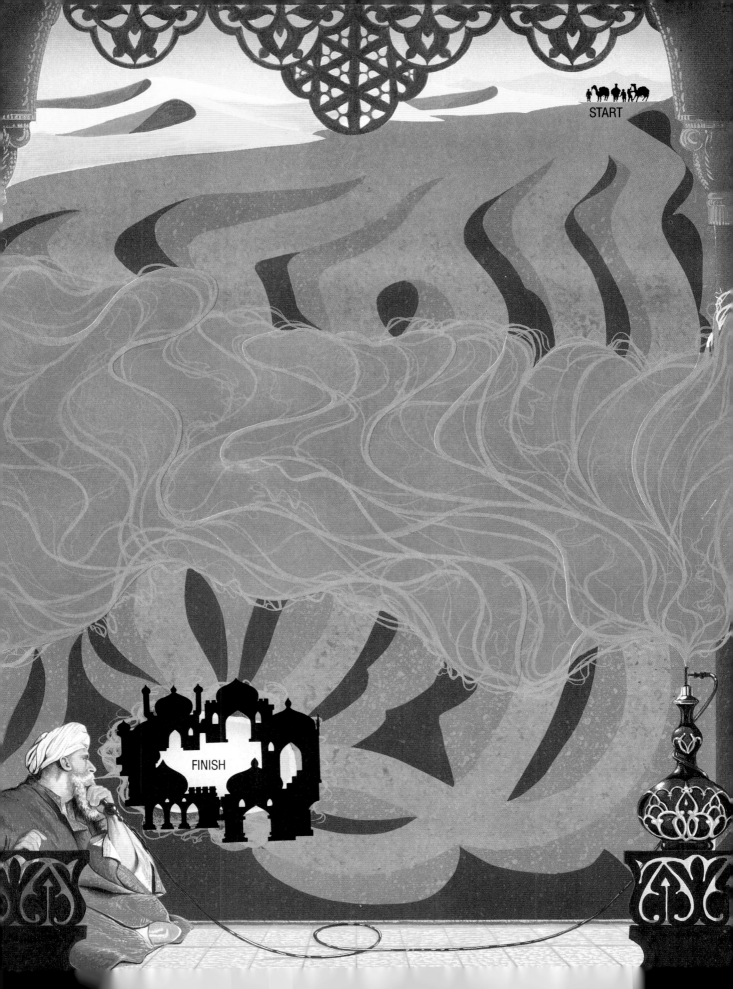

START

FINISH

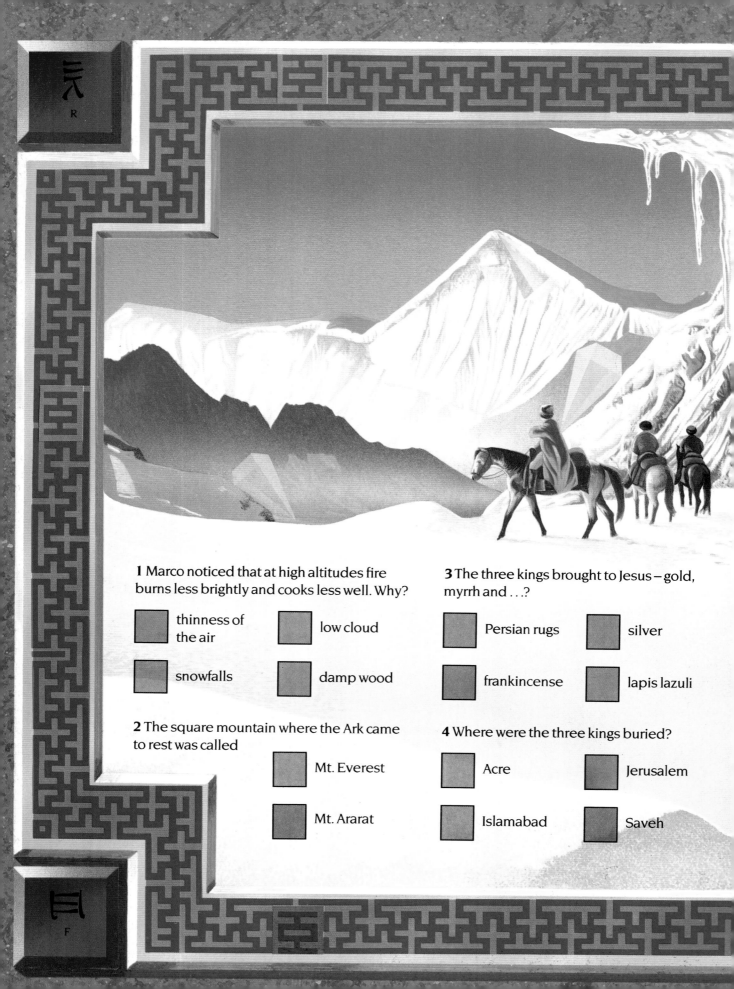

1 Marco noticed that at high altitudes fire burns less brightly and cooks less well. Why?

☐ thinness of the air

☐ low cloud

☐ snowfalls

☐ damp wood

2 The square mountain where the Ark came to rest was called

☐ Mt. Everest

☐ Mt. Ararat

3 The three kings brought to Jesus – gold, myrrh and . . .?

☐ Persian rugs

☐ silver

☐ frankincense

☐ lapis lazuli

4 Where were the three kings buried?

☐ Acre

☐ Jerusalem

☐ Islamabad

☐ Saveh

Leaving Persia, the Venetians travelled to Balkh, in Afghanistan. Here the road divided. They decided to take the shortest, but highest way to China. This led eastwards over the Pamir Mountains into Chinese Turkestan.

The three travellers set off eastwards and reached the Pamirs, the "Roof of the World", where several great mountain ranges met.

After three days' climbing, they reached the grassy plains high among the mountains. Marco saw large wild sheep, with curly horns, grazing there. Later, these were given the scientific name O*vis poli* (Polo's sheep) in his honor.

5 How many gems can you see hidden in the scene above?

8	6
10	15

Marco and the intrepid travellers take a brief rest to view the scenery. Set **Super Q** *to Mode* **3F** *and find the five holy symbols hidden in the design of the border. The symbols are shaped like this:* 至
Also answer the five questions. (You have 3 minutes.)

START

FINISH

Arriving at Kashgar, the three travellers had reached the fringes of China. But there was still far to go before reaching the court of Kublai Khan. The biggest obstacle to their journey was now the terrible Gobi Desert.

Not only was the Gobi barren and hostile, it was said to be haunted. If, crossing the desert, a man became separated from his companions, he would hear evil spirits, calling him with the voices of his friends. If he followed the voices, he would become totally lost . . .

Set **Super Q** to Mode **4H** and spot the hidden route through the desert to safety. If you make more than four mistakes, the spirits will lead Marco astray. You must find all 40 steps to complete the journey properly.

Z

The Mystery in Tangut

Despite these stories, the Venetians safely crossed the Gobi in 30 days.

On the other side of the desert, they came to a region which produced a strange mineral called salamander. Marco wrote that this was not an animal as Europeans thought, but a mineral fiber which could be spun into a cloth. This cloth would not burn, but turned white when put into a fire. (Today, this mineral is known as asbestos; it was used for fire-proofing until it was realized that its fibers are dangerous to the lungs.)

As soon as the Venetians reached Tangut, messengers rode off to Kublai Khan. An escort met them and conducted them to Kublai Khan's Summer Palace, which was at Shang-tu, in Mongolia. They arrived there after a 40-day journey. it was now the summer of 1275. The Venetians had been travelling for more than three years.

*Marco is tired and thirsty, and has dropped his water bottle somewhere in the sand. Set **Super Q** to Mode **4A** and answer the eight questions to help him find it; make more than two mistakes, and he can go no further.*

The Sheikh of The Mountain

On his travels, Marco heard a strange story about a bygone ruler called the Sheikh of the mountain.

This Sheikh built a secret garden in a hidden mountain valley, which he filled with fine fruit trees, fountains running with wine and a beautiful dancing girls. At his court he kept an army of young men.

He would give a sleeping potion to ten or twenty men at a time, and have them taken, while asleep, to the secret garden. When they awoke they believed they were in Paradise, and never wanted to leave. The Sheikh would let them stay there until he needed some of them to attack his enemies. Then he had the chosen youths put to sleep again and brought back to his palace. The Sheikh sent them off to fight, with the promise that, if they succeeded, they would return to Paradise.

These youths were called the Assassins.

1 Marco was born in 1254 AD and left Venice when he was 15. How old was he in 1282?

- [ ] 32
- [ ] 28
- [ ] 38
- [ ] 22

2 The camel's ability to go long periods without water, and its special hooves have earned it the nickname of

- [ ] old reliable
- [ ] ship of the desert

3 Real pearls are rare. What animals create them?

- [ ] jellyfish
- [ ] oysters

4 Oil, coal and natural gas are created by compressed decayed matter. What are these known as?

- [ ] compressed fuel
- [ ] fossil fuel

5 Marco was enthralled by Persia. What is it called now?

- [ ] Babylon
- [ ] Iran
- [ ] Beirut
- [ ] Iraq

6 Kublai Khan ruled China for many years but was not Chinese. What was he?

- [ ] Mormon
- [ ] Mongol
- [ ] Tibetan
- [ ] Pekinese

7 Kublai Khan was one of nine grandsons to a famous warrior. Who was his grandfather?

- [ ] Myokin Khan
- [ ] Genghis Khan
- [ ] Khanet Khan
- [ ] Genkho Khan

8 The Chinese have used silk for centuries. Where does it come from?

- [ ] bushes
- [ ] sheep
- [ ] caterpillars

START ▶

U

Kublai Khan greeted the travellers warmly. They gave him gifts from the pope, and the holy oil from Jerusalem. Nicolo presented his son to the emperor. Kublai was impressed by Marco and took him into his service. Marco was now aged 22.

Kublai Khan's messengers used a relay system to send messages back to the palace. Set **Super Q** *to Mode* **8A** *and get the important news of Marco's arrival to the emperor. You have 15 seconds.*

FINISH

Majestic Hunt

The Venetians stayed at Shang-tu for the rest of the summer months, and took part in the hunting trips which were the emperor's favorite pastime.

According to Marco, the hunt was accompanied by thousands of falconers who set loose falcons, hawks and other hunting birds in search of prey. Thousands more look-outs blew whistles to call back the birds and hood them.

As Kublai Khan was getting on in years and suffered from gout (from too much drink) he did not take an active part. Instead, he was carried along on a couch in a luxurious cabin on the backs of four elephants. The cabin was lined with gold cloth inside and draped with lion skins outside. When his servants warned that birds such as cranes were near, he would draw a curtain aside and watch his falcons swoop on the birds.

For hunting deer the emperor used trained cheetahs and lynxes, as well as dogs. The cheetahs rode along on the backs of horses, following their keepers.

After the hunt, Kublai and his nobles would relax in a collection of tents and pavilions, described by Marco as being a small city.

*The hunt is on! Marco is riding a sleek mount at the head of the hunting party. Set **Super Q** to Mode **3B**. Help him spot six animals native to China and answer the questions in two minutes.*

1 Pandas, an endangered species, prefer

☐ honey ☐ bamboo shoots ☐ lychees

2 What is the fastest that a hunting cheetah can run?

☐ 20-25mph ☐ 70-80mph ☐ 60-65mph

Each year, at the end of August, Kublai Khan returned to his new capital, Peking (then called Khanbalik). The new city was planned like a number of Chinese boxes, one inside the next and crisscrossed with streets at right angles. The outer walls formed an oblong. Inside this, another set of walls enclosed the palace grounds, and a third set of walls enclosed the palace itself. The emperor's palace was built of marble and stood on platforms which raised it above the level of the city. It contained 400 rooms, richly painted in gold, silver and blue.

In Peking, no-one is allowed out after dusk. The curfew bell has sounded and Marco is not home. He must get back to the safety of his room, avoiding the guards.
Set **Super Q** to Mode **8C** and find his way in 45 seconds.

START

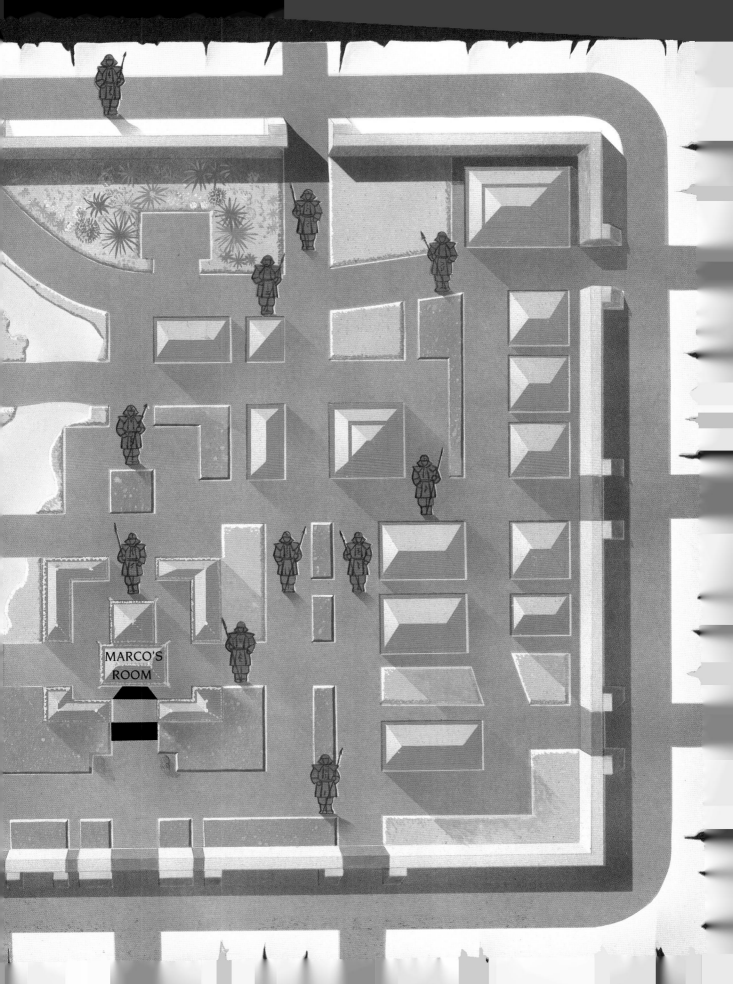

Emperor's Embezzler

Kublai Khan quickly realized that Marco was intelligent and trustworthy, and took him into his favor. Marco worked hard to learn the four main languages spoken in China, and the emperor began to entrust him with important government work.

Marco's first mission for Kublai Khan was to travel to Burma as an ambassador for the Mongols, whom the Burmese were trying to keep out of their country. This journey took three-and-a-half months. In Burma, Marco picked up all the information he could, and sent it back to the emperor.

Later, Kublai Khan made Marco governor of the important and wealthy city of Yangchau. This was because he thought that Marco, a foreigner who was not a Mongol, would be more acceptable to the Chinese people of the city. Marco governed Yangchau for three years.

The Polos were useful to the emperor in other ways. The city of Siang-yang-fu refused to submit to Mongol rule, and held out against Kublai Khan's army for three years. The Polos then told the Mongols how to build siege engines to hurl boulders into the city. This was done, and the city promptly surrendered.

Marco was impressed by the use of paper money in China, centuries before it was used in Europe. It was made from mulberry bark, and stamped with the emperor's seal in red ink, at his mint in Peking.

*Marco is tallying the accounts of a nobleman suspected of embezzling imperial funds. Set **Super Q** to Mode **4A** and, using the key, find which seven sums are wrong by pressing **Super Q** on their totals. Then answer the question in the box at the end. Do not make more than two errors; the emperor is anxious for a result...*

| 1 | 2 | 3 | 4 | 5 | 6 | 7 | 8 | 9 | 0 |

A

I

The nobleman
was...

an embezzler

bad at sums

H

D

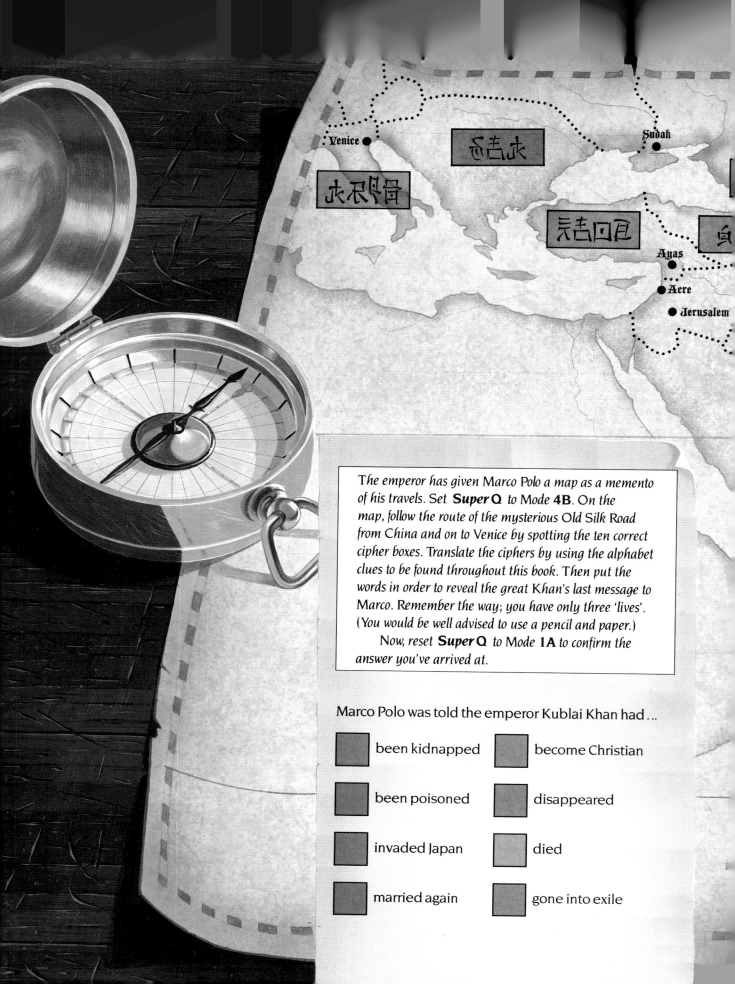

The emperor has given Marco Polo a map as a memento of his travels. Set **SuperQ** to Mode **4B**. On the map, follow the route of the mysterious Old Silk Road from China and on to Venice by spotting the ten correct cipher boxes. Translate the ciphers by using the alphabet clues to be found throughout this book. Then put the words in order to reveal the great Khan's last message to Marco. Remember the way; you have only three 'lives'. (You would be well advised to use a pencil and paper.)

Now, reset **SuperQ** to Mode **1A** to confirm the answer you've arrived at.

Marco Polo was told the emperor Kublai Khan had...

	been kidnapped		become Christian
	been poisoned		disappeared
	invaded Japan		died
	married again		gone into exile

The Return

After 17 years in China, the three Venetians felt that they would like to return home to Venice. Kublai Khan was growing old, and they feared what might happen when he died. But when they asked permission to leave, the emperor refused. He was too fond of the Venetians and Marco was too useful as his trusted servant.

Then, three ambassadors arrived from Persia, where there was also a Mongol ruler. This king's wife had died, and he wished to marry a Mongol princess from China, from the same family as his wife. It was arranged that the princess Kokachin would travel back to Persia with the ambassadors.

Because of the dangers of the return journey to Persia, the ambassadors asked Kublai Khan to allow the three Venetians to go with them. Reluctantly the emperor agreed, but made the Venetians promise to return. A fleet of ships was fitted out, and the party set sail from China in 1292.

The journey to Persia took about two years, with many hardships on the way. When the Venetians arrived there, they heard that Kublai Khan had died. So, after safely delivering the princess, the Polos decided not to return to China, and made their way back to Venice.

They finally arrived in Venice in 1295, 24 years after they had left it. Marco Polo and his father and uncle had probably travelled over more of the world than anyone before.

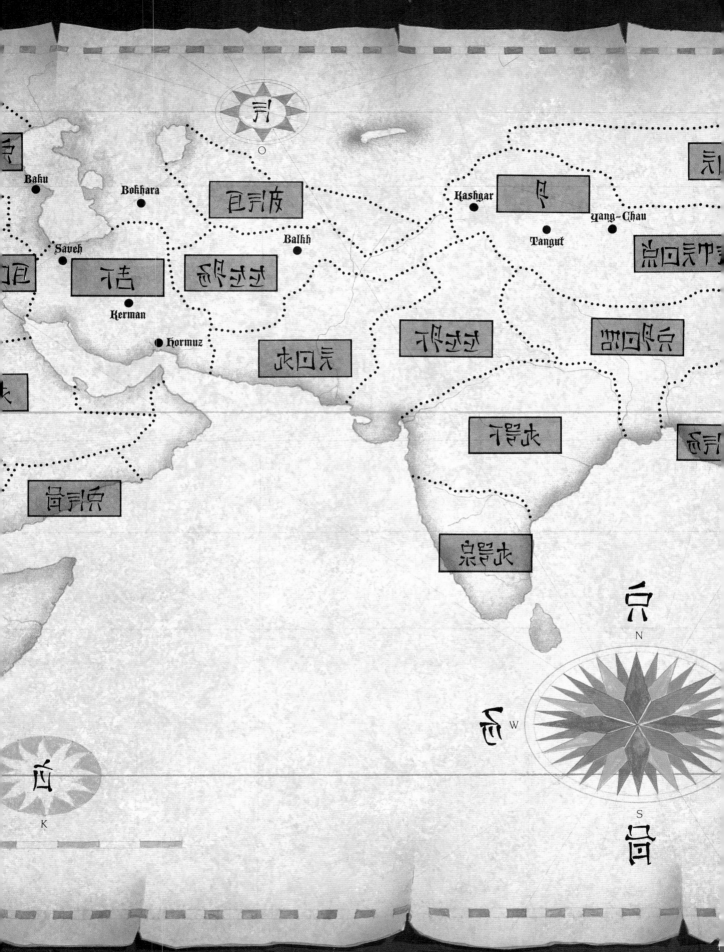

Epilogue

About a year after returning home, Marco became the commander of a Venetian galley, and was captured in a sea battle against Venice's rival city, Genoa. The Genoans kept him prisoner for three years.

Among Marco's fellow-prisoners was a man from Pisa, one Rustichello, a writer. He was fascinated by Marco's stories, and they agreed to make a book about them.

Marco was allowed home for his travel notes, and they set to work. Written at first in French, the book was finished in 1298, and it has been famous ever since, in many translations.

In 1299 Genoa and Venice made peace. Marco was freed and returned to Venice. Soon afterwards, Rustichello was also freed. Marco Polo lived the rest of his life quietly in Venice, where he died, aged 70, in 1324.